BARACK OBAMA

A Little Golden Book® Biography

By Frank Berrios
Illustrated by Kristin Sorra

A GOLDEN BOOK • NEW YORK

Text copyright © 2022 by Frank Berrios
Cover art and interior illustrations copyright © 2022 by Kristin Sorra
All rights reserved. Published in the United States by Golden Books, an imprint of Random
House Children's Books, a division of Penguin Random House LLC, 1745 Broadway, New York,
NY 10019. Golden Books, A Golden Book, A Little Golden Book, the G colophon, and
the distinctive gold spine are registered trademarks of Penguin Random House LLC.
rhcbooks.com
Educators and librarians, for a variety of teaching tools, visit us at RHTeachersLibrarians.com
Library of Congress Control Number: 2021941292
ISBN 978-0-593-47936-0 (trade) — ISBN 978-0-593-47937-7 (ebook)
Printed in the United States of America
10 9 8 7 6 5 4

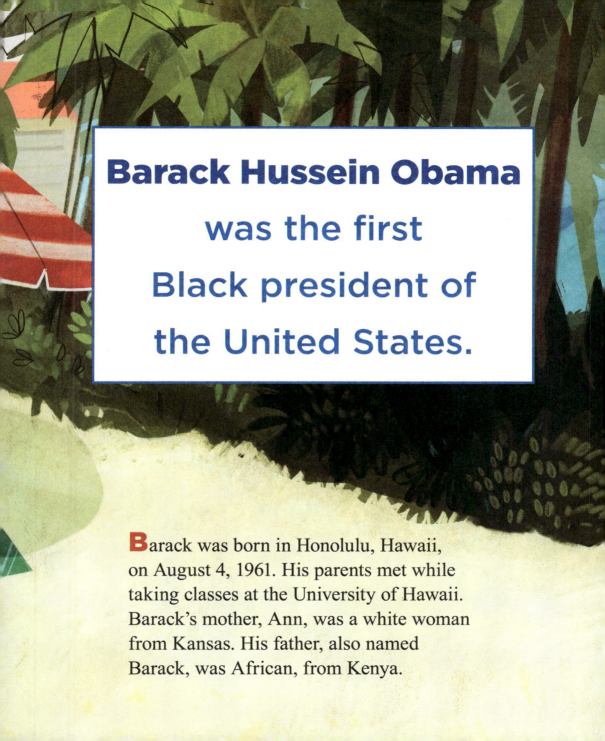

Barack Hussein Obama

was the first Black president of the United States.

Barack was born in Honolulu, Hawaii, on August 4, 1961. His parents met while taking classes at the University of Hawaii. Barack's mother, Ann, was a white woman from Kansas. His father, also named Barack, was African, from Kenya.

During this time in America, it was illegal in several states for a white person to marry a Black person. Thankfully, those laws did not exist in Hawaii, where people of many different cultures lived together peacefully.

ALL DEPARTURE GATES ↗

When Barack was just two years old, his father left Hawaii to attend Harvard University in Massachusetts. Barack's parents found it difficult to be so far apart. After a few years, the young couple divorced.

Soon, Barack's mom met and married another man. His name was Lolo, and he was from Indonesia. Ann and Barack moved there to live with Lolo.

Indonesia was exciting to Barack, who was called Barry. His backyard was filled with chickens, ducks, and two baby crocodiles. Barry even had a pet ape!

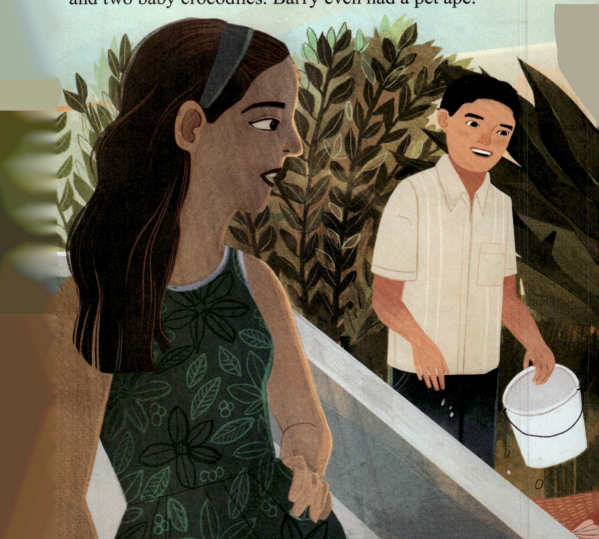

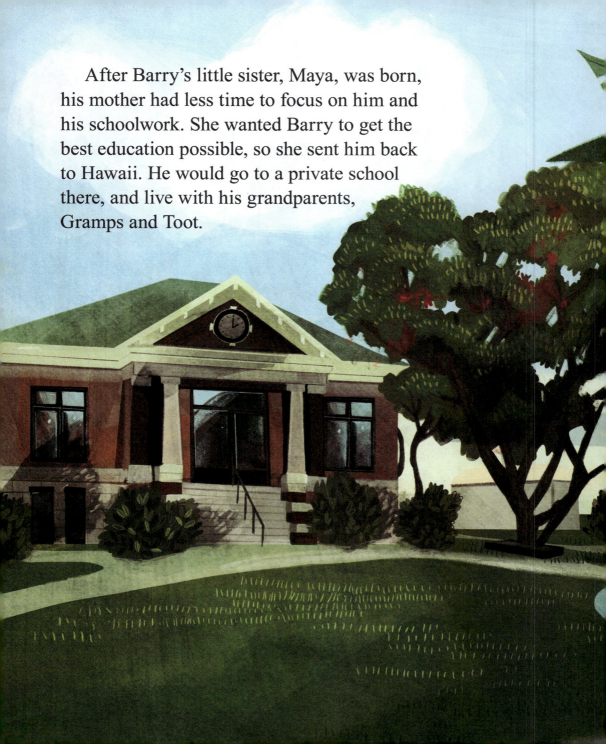

After Barry's little sister, Maya, was born, his mother had less time to focus on him and his schoolwork. She wanted Barry to get the best education possible, so she sent him back to Hawaii. He would go to a private school there, and live with his grandparents, Gramps and Toot.

Later that year, Barry's father came to visit and was asked to give a speech at his school. Barry's classmates were excited to hear about Kenya, and all the amazing things to see and do in Africa.

After his father's speech,
Barry became prouder of
his African heritage.

Although he was very smart, Barry didn't always do well in school. But he was a friendly and popular student, as well as one of the better players on his high school basketball team.

When Barry graduated from high school, he went to Occidental College in Los Angeles, and then to Columbia University in New York City. Around this time, he also decided to drop his nickname. Now everyone called him Barack.

Although Barack hadn't seen his father since he was ten, they kept in touch. His father even invited him to visit their family in Kenya. But before Barack could make the trip, his father passed away.

Barack finally went to Kenya a few years after he graduated from college. He was excited to meet his sister and brothers, cousins, aunts, and uncles!

After a few weeks, Barack returned to the United States and began studying law at Harvard, where he eventually became the first Black president of the Harvard Law Review.

The summer after his first year at the school, he worked at a law firm in Chicago, and met a smart and lovely lawyer named Michelle Robinson. The two dated and soon fell in love!

After graduating from law school, Barack wrote a book about his life called *Dreams from My Father*. He began teaching at the University of Chicago Law School.

As a civil rights lawyer, Barack worked with people who had been treated unfairly at home or at work simply because of the color of their skin.

In 1992, Barack and Michelle got married. Not long after, their first daughter, Malia, was born, followed three years later by Sasha.

Barack enjoyed his new life as a husband and father, but he wanted to do more for his community. As a lawyer, he saw firsthand how some laws hurt people instead of helping them. In 1996, Barack was elected to the Illinois Senate. He wanted to create new laws to help people find good jobs and homes.

In 2004, Barack won a seat in the U.S. Senate. Many people had never heard of him, but he was asked to give the keynote speech at the Democratic National Convention that year. People across the country were inspired by his stirring words of hope for a better America.

Barack began his presidential campaign in 2007, and selected Joe Biden as his vice president. He hoped the country was ready for change. On November 4, 2008, Barack made history when he was elected the 44th president of the United States of America!

Barack started helping the country right away. Many people had lost their jobs, so he created new jobs to help get them back to work. To keep Americans healthy, Barack fought for and approved the Affordable Care Act in 2010. Then Barack made history again when he was elected for a second term as president in 2012!

Barack left the White House in 2017, but his work continues. He has written more books. He donates his time and money to causes that lift people up and bring them together. And he inspires people around the world to take action and make changes in their lives for a better and brighter future!